Dr. Chuckle and Missed Her Ride

Puns and Malapropisms

Puns and Malapropisms

Dr. Chuckle and Missed Her Ride

Paul Frishkoff

Wild ginger Press

ISBN: 978-0-9960785-3-5

Cover design, book design and production by Bobbi Benson, Wild Ginger Press.
www.wildgingerpress.com

In memory of
Lou ("Louie") Johns, who had a deep laugh
and even deeper insights.

CONTENTS

Paul, in the midst of Worf-fare,
teaching his last class at the
University of Oregon.

Photo by Pat Frishkoff

PREFACE

To Humor
It May Concern

A DYSLEXIC RETIRED millwright walks into … "A Course in Miracles" study group.

Among the half-dozen regular study group attendees, there was I. Despite his dyslexia and limited vision in one eye, Lou Johns didn't hesitate to read aloud when it was his turn. (I later found out that he'd taught a number of illiterate people how to read.) Lou was gifted with humor, laughter and a profound sense of acceptance and forgiveness. As his lung cancer worsened, he invited friends to his adult baptism and anointment ceremony. One day, a pun popped into my head, and I thought to myself, "Lou will like that."

So I saved it, along with many other puns. Lou left us before I could share my collection with him, but I've continued amassing puns, and now they've been gathered into the book that you hold in your hands.

There are no one-person books, any more than there are one-actor plays. I might not have gone forward with this project without the encouragement of my wife, Pat, who has been forced to be an audience of one for all my jokes over the years, especially since I left academia. Close friends have expressed bemusement or at least tolerance when I told them what I was writing. My late mentor, Dan Jones, modeled joy for me. While I was stumbling around in search of a knowledgeable book person, I had the great fortune to meet, by chance, Bobbi Benson, who has served as Creative Director for this book and has seen it through from concept to finished product. The book was ably and painstakingly edited by Erin J. Bernard.

The manuscript was painstakingly checked by Pru Frieda. Font selection was by the Serif of Rottingham. The guinea pigs who patiently listened to my puns over and over, were: Cody Pendant, Sophie Ring and Bart Ender. My page numberer was Noah C. Quince. The indexer was Doane Bother. My anonymity quality control person is Sue DeNimme. Our footnoting, offshored to Krakow, was by Opcitz Zatrak. Damaged copies of the book were ably repaired by Anita Mendes-Pine. The consulting copyright attorney is Seymour Loopholes. The Las Vegas book-signing and gambling junket was arranged by the Cashew Inn.

Foreword march!

INTRODUCTION

THE FIRST PUN I REMEMBER from my childhood was by the comedian Henry Morgan, who joked about "The Loan Arranger" (a play on "The Lone Ranger"). My father – also named Lou – was more of an able raconteur than a punster, but my equally weird brother, Bruce, and I have exchanged zingers – a kind of mutually appreciative verbal ping-pong – since forever. Auditory humor appeals to me, whereas purely visual humor such as mime tends to escape me. I have a particular admiration for the late cartoonist Walt Kelly. His comic strip, *Pogo*, had a richness of wordplay that went beyond what one might expect from a gifted cartoon artist.

I hope that readers enjoy (at least some of) the puns that make up the first part of this book. I certainly enjoyed crafting them.

Over the course of my long professorial career at the University of Oregon Lundquist College of Business, I taught several thousand students. It was my great pleasure, and the second part of the book contains a series of malapropisms (along with some bloopers and misused cognates) collected from term papers that I corrected through the years. Like Mrs. Malaprop, a character in playwright Richard Brinsley Sheridan's "The Rivals," my students' occasional misuse of words and phrases resulted in what might be considered *inadvertent* puns. The excerpts are given verbatim, except when a change was necessary to protect anonymity. I'd like to stress that I have the utmost respect and fondness for students. I corrected their errors gently, and I certainly didn't pass along the sardonic comments that I've appended to each malapropism in this book.

To help you along your way as you read through this collection, here's a hint: if you don't "get" a pun or malapropism on the first pass, *read the answer aloud.* Enjoy.

Puns

Food

Warning: "Consuming too many of these puns
in a sitting can cause irritable vowel!"
~ GUS TATORI, MD

Why did Jeffrey Dahmer's antique car smell
like cinnamon rolls?
He Studebaker.

Why did the chef serve thin soup to his girlfriend?
To consommé the relationship.

What musical soundtrack is used in Beano commercials?
Taco Bell's Cannon.

4

What's for lunch at the House of Usher?

Poe-boy sandwiches.

5

Who concocted thousands of recipes for broad beans,
and what else is he known for?

*Dr. George Washington Fava; he was
"The Fava of His Country."*

6

When's the best time to gulp a latte?

When the swallows come back to Cappuccino.

7

Why didn't Sherlock Holmes season his food with basil?

It irritated his wrath-bone!

8

What's the byproduct of eating too much beans and rice?

The Creature from the Black Legume.

What happened to the Tibetan who was allergic to milk?

He came down with self-yak disease.

What do galley slaves eat for lunch?

Whipped roe and fetter cheese.

11

Why do stoners make good chefs?

They're frying by the seeds of their plants.

12

What did the waiter say when the diner
complained of greasy meat?

"Suet yourself."

Where do you learn to cook dumplings al dente?

The School of Hard Gnocchi.

Where do histrionic people drink camel milk?
At the Drama Dairy.

What do male porn stars drink?
Oolong tea.

What's the newest fertility food?
Quints jam.

Gnocchi-gnocchi. Who's-a-There?
Rigatoni. Rigatoni who?
Let's party in Riga, Tony!

Why is an abacus used at Chinese restaurants?
To arrive at a dim sum.

What did the pharaoh and his retinue do
after their bean dinner?

They had a Tutankhamen.

What did Don Quixote eat in the desert?

Manna La Mancha.

21

Why did the shepherd assail his wife's recipe?

He liked his lambasted.

22

What do you get from cabbage at airport eateries?

Terminal farts.

23

What did Reverend Spooner recommend
for hotdog condiments?

Pay Groupon.

24

What did the spice merchant do every May?

He sent a cardamom.

Music and Art

*"Reading more than one will make your
three-cornered hat shoot off your head."*
~ MANUAL DEFILER

What do extroverted priests sing?
Gregarious chants.

How was Lawrence Welk compensated?
With polka chips.

Who stole the Vatican's jazz CD collection?
Felonious Monk.

What do mariachi bands play on St. Patrick's Day?

"How Are Things in Guacamole?"

How did Rossini woo women?

He made overtures to them.

Who played the dirge at the tightrope walker's funeral?

A nonet.

Which opera inspired the inventor of d-CON?

"Deflate-a-mouse."

How did the bottomless performer become wealthy?

She created a bun dance.

33

What do beatniks do in the Fourth of July parade?

They form a hip, hip, hip array.

34

What was St. Francis's favorite song?

"Assisi to remember, and so hard to forget."

35

Which musician was named for his unstable mother?

Yo Yo Ma.

36

Who attends musicals in the nude?

Theatre buffs.

37

Why was the jazz bassist indicted?

He was playing with his pianist in public.

How did the percussion player become
such a good angler?

He knew how to castanet.

Which line dance is done by Flemish beer-swiggers?

The belchin' conga.

What made Mingus quit his high-school band?

He couldn't get to first bass.

Why do Neapolitans like to drool in their bean pasta
and dance tarantella?

That's the mores.

Why did the reggae singer have a mistrial?

The jury was dreadlocked.

43

What's the biggest Norwegian love song?

"Olaf me, why not take Olaf me?"

44

What tune do dairy farmers hum?

"In the Mooed."

45

Why is it so easy to become a lap dancer?

It ain't exactly Rockette science!

46

Who are the up-and-coming Mongolian punk rockers?

The Gobi Tweens.

47

What's the riskiest move for majorettes?

The Baton Death March.

48

What's a diorama?

The wages of Cinerama.

49

Who composes show tunes in Kuwait?

Tin Pan Ali.

50

What did the glee club share before snorkeling?

A choral reefer.

51

What happened when the orchestra went on strike?

The audience found it disconcerting.

52

Who vandalized the modern glass museum?

Chibulygans.

What woodwind do sadists play?

The flageolet.

Who painted "Crossing the Ceiling in Toledo"?

El Gecko.

Which movies feature gamelan music?

*"Gong with the Wind," "Miss Saigong,"
"Gong-a-Din," "King Gong,"
"Top Gong," "Gongs of New York."*

Which hue do third-rate artists prefer?

Medi-ochre.

What did the sarcastic writer use in Novi Sad?

A Serb Bic.

58

What did Bach say to the nasty music critic?

"Go fugue yourself!"

Animals and Other Critters

"These are the origin of the specious."
~ JONATHAN LIVINGSTON BEAGLE

59

What voyeur lurks on coral reefs?

Anemone of the peephole.

60

Why are ambulance chasers such rats?

They came up through the "sue her" system.

61

How did Tarzan become friends with Cheetah?

or: They were both swingers.

He took him as a gibbon, or: He was a chimp off the old block,

What motivated the rancher to catch the rustlers?

His cattle list.

Where did Noah learn about the birds and the bees?

He looked in his ark hives.

Why do people detest lice?

They're pubic enemy #1.

Who was trampled while putting I.D. tags on pigs?

An innocent sty-bander.

Did you hear the one about the magician,
the nun and the rodent?

He pulled a habit out of the rat.

What does the whale shark eat?

It inhales reefers.

What caused that rutting sound in the bamboo forest?

Panda-moan-yum.

Which moralists wallow in African rivers?

Hippo critters.

Which bird is scared to go down on her mate and why?

The yellow-bellied sapsucker. (Because he has a wood pecker.)

What hindered the witches' picnic?

Coven-ants.

What do camels leave behind after grazing?
The chips of the desert.

Who is the stoutest camel in the Gobi?
Humpty-Dumpy.

How did Lassie die?
From E. collie poisoning.

75

What do pigs do at the ballpark?
They root, root for the home team.

76

What do you call a sociopathic mastodon?
A sycophant.

What's the past tense of the word "seahorse"?

Sawhorse.

Why do Lithuanian men scratch their crotches?

Ball-ticks.

Why were the Siamese cats insulted
by their role in the film?

They were cast as Persians.

Spirituality and Religion

*"Immoderate consumption of these puns
might put you into a stupa."*
~ THE JOLLY LAMA

80

In Rouen, how do they refer to Joan of Arc?

As the "Toast" of the town.

81

Why did the Dalai Lama appear on "Wheel of Fortune"?

He wanted to get near Vanna.

82

What do you call Reverend Roberts' passionate followers?

Oral's sects.

Who washes his hands before exercising?

Pontius Pilates.

In which Old Testament book does Goliath slay David?

The Philistine Prophecy.

Why did people join the Crusades?

March madness!

Who foresees the tides in Nova Scotia?

The Fundy mentalists.

Did you hear about the Buddhist hair salon?

They don't do permanents.

88

How did St. Peter acquire hemorrhoids?
He was a big fissure man.

89

What happened to the sinful monk?
He fell into the abbess.

90

Why do clergymen take Cialis?
For res-erection.

91

Who announces when Judgment Day's arrived?
The Four Horsemen of the Apostrophe.

92

Why didn't the agnostic run for public office?
He declined denomination.

93

What do you get if you cross John Wesley
and Marie Curie?
A Scientific Methodist.

94

Why was the parish flooded with complaints when the
bishop was caught with the novice?
He was in-nun-dated.

95

How did the dyslexic find religion?
By using savior-faire.

96

What's the lesson of the Good Samaritan parable?
There's a succor born every minute.

97

Who fearlessly parks cars where evil lurks?
The Valet of the Shadow.

98

Why was Martin Luther always constipated,
and how did it affect his oratory?

He had a Diet of Worms; and he spoke with baited breath.

History and Literature

"Ingesting these too rapidly may cause great expectorations."
~ SAL IVAR

99

Who were the earliest primitive nomads?

The Meanderthals.

100

What do cannibals do in the Emerald City?

They munch kin.

101

Who was Genghis Khan's Eurasian camp follower?

The Mongrel Whore.

On what TV show did call girls do "The Wave"?

"Tsunami Vice."

What did the Athenians say when Archimedes
farted in the public bath?

"You reek, ugh!"

Why was Michael Corleone so rigid and quick to shoot?

He was a hard Don.

Whose proboscis grew longer when he lied to juries,
and why was it so long in the first place?

Cyranose de Perjurac; it ran in the family.

106

Why did Prince Charming win over Cinderella?

The ball was in his court.

How did Marco Polo describe his journey to China?

"My Mongolian Iliad."

How did Jack the Ripper kill so many hookers?

He was the "offer" they couldn't refuse.

Who was guillotined for indecent exposure?

Disrobes-Pierre.

What did Cicero proclaim as he ate fried eel?

"O tempura, o morays!"

What did the Incas call their annual pissing contest?

The Macho Pee-shoot.

112

What was the downfall of the last of the Mohicans?

He took up the White Man's bourbon.

113

From what did Van Gogh suffer?

Excess ear whacks.

114

Did you hear about the sociopathic Santa?

*He loves to slay belles, and he'll seize you
when you're sleeping.*

115

How do gods ascend in Greek tragedies?

They use Aeschyl-ators.

116

What did Euclid do with his girlfriend?

He worked on his log-rythms.

What were Dr. Jekyll's downfalls?

He never medicine he didn't like, and he could run but he couldn't Hyde.

Where did Jack Frost make it with the Ice Queen?

In the boar house.

What destroyed Pompeii?

Eruptile dysfunction.

In which style did Adam write prose?

In the first person.

What did the sheriff's friends say when he belched?

"Wyatt Earp?"

122

Who wore tuxedos as the Titanic sank?

Ocean swells.

123

Why did Robinson Crusoe need a banker?

He wanted to float alone.

124

Who invented masturbation?

John Handcock, or Onan the Barbarian.

125

How long was Theseus stuck in the labyrinth?

A Minotaur two.

126

Who plays the minor parts in the movie, "Wall Street"?

Stock characters.

What made the captain of the Titanic so swellheaded?

He had the wrong capsize.

128

Who used to decide what was fitting for America?

J. Edgar Behoover.

129

Who was too slow on the throttle?

The Boston Straggler.

130

How did Jacob Marley spend Christmas Eves?

Delivering chain letters.

131

What became of the Wicked Witch?

She turned to ooze in Oz.

Why did Albert Schweitzer always get on top of his wife?
He was a missionary-physician.

What did Mark Antony say about
recent pyramid schemes?
"Ambition should be Madoff sterner stuff!"

What did Edison do when his filament finally worked?
He became lightheaded.

Where did Venetian doges show off their equipment?
On the Bridge of Size.

Who was the most boring poet?
"T.D.S." Eliot.

Why did Cinderella's stepmother drop her off the roof?

She didn't like to hold on to drudges.

Who rose from poverty by doing research on hookers?

Whore-ratio Alger.

What did the English professor value
more than his majors?

His privates.

What did Cratchit dream of doing to Scrooge?

Shooting his tightwad.

What killed Cleopatra?

E-reptile dysfunction.

142

What did ocean waves do to Kon-Tiki?

Raised the rafters.

143

Who polices the waterfront at night, and how
do they detect waterfront meth labs?

The dockside of the Force; from chemical wharf air.

144

How did the English defeat the Spanish Armada?

The got more miles per galleon.

145

Which assassin wrote erotic stories,
and why were they funny?

Anaïs Ninja; because she had a sensei of humor.

146

Why were the Mafioso's memoirs a best seller?

He was an author who couldn't be refused.

Celebrities and Superheroes

*"If I'd known that I'd live this long, I'd have read
these more slowly – and prayed more."*
~ MICKEY MANTIS

What are the chances that Kate Moss will
be the next Mother Teresa?
Slim and nun.

What does Al Sharpton do at Churchill Downs?
Plays the race card.

What happened to Superman when
he swallowed kryptonite?

He's in a crypt tonight!

What did Jerry Lewis say to Salvador Dali?

"Are you surreal?"

Why wouldn't Howard Hughes use public toilets?

They were within his fear of effluents.

Who located John Bobbitt's missing "appendage"?

Dick Tracy.

153

What did Dr. Ruth say about premature ejaculation?

"It can be a real shortcoming!"

Why did O.J. Simpson bring a knife to the inquest?

To cut coroners.

What did Mr. Cobb do in 1961?

Ty died.

To what did Princess Di succumb?

Carpool tunnel syndrome.

What was The Shadow's tribal ancestry?

The In-Visigoths.

What did Superman do when he became destitute?

He peddled his S.

What did The Shadow say about spam?

"Who knows what email irks?"

160

Why did Aunt Jemima go to the doctor?

For her mammy-gram.

Science and Medicine

"Take one and call me in the mourning."
~ DR. SMOCK

Who takes Viagra at Sing Sing?
Only hardened criminals.

Who soaks up IT information like a blotter?
Absorber the Geek.

Why are there so many octogenarian eye doctors?
They dilate.

164

Why did the Alaskan conceal his dyslexia?

He was in Denali.

165

What do statisticians do with their hostages?

They hold them for random.

166

Who sells pirated software on the streets of Calcutta?

Seedy Ram.

167

What did the constipated pirate say?

"Argonaut!"

168

Why did they strip-search the old lady for plutonium?

They were looking for every nuke in Granny.

Why did the grammar fanatic have a heart attack?

She was past tense.

Why do eye doctors finish last in comedy contests?

They tell cornea jokes.

What did the statistician and her hunk
achieve in the back seat?

Car-elation.

Where do volcanologists do their best thinking?

In their lava-tories.

Why do cardiologists skip golf in emergencies?

They put the heart before the course.

What degree do volcanologists hold?

Magma come louder.

Why did the mummy consult his gastroenterologist?

About his ruptured sarcophagus.

What's a urologist's favorite Christmas carol?

"God Rest Ye Merry Genital Men."

What did the cardiac surgeon say when he
botched the operation?

"Aorta know better!"

Did you hear about the lecherous birdwatcher?
What was his greatest triumph?

He was a pornithologist; it was his night-in-Gail.

Why did the accountant become a psychologist?

Many of her clients were unbalanced.

Racy and Raunchy

"If elation lasts more than four hours, call your mirthologist."
~ DR. FILL

Whose bright idea was fetishism?

Plato's?

What are you guaranteed if caught whizzing in public?

A jury of your pee-ers.

Why are freeway shoulders littered
with discarded condoms?

It's "where the rubber meets the road."

What did Daddy Warbucks say while he groped Annie?

"Do you come here, orphan?"

Who giggles when he pokes you?

The Pillsbury Dildo Boy.

Who gave the initial approval to sell Viagra?

The Surgin' Genital.

Where do you find able-bodied semen?

It comes in gobs.

What do toreros use instead of K-Y Jelly?

Oil of Olé.

188

Why aren't eunuchs more popular?

They're low men on the scrotum poll.

189

How is lovemaking among the Bedouins?

It can often be in tents.

190

What did the judge tell the statutory rapist?

"You felon her!"

191

Why don't parachutists wear briefs?

They enjoy in-descent exposure.

192

Why was the lecher so hush-hush about his conquest?

He was on the cutie!

What raises the birthrate down in Georgia?

Macon whoopee.

What did the Braille-reader do with the thin woman?

Svelte her up.

What did the Afghani say to his bed partner?

"You Pushtu!"

How did the dictator maintain population growth?

He had the rubber banned.

Why do adult theaters show cartoons
between porn flicks?

It's the inter-lewd.

What happened when the shining local hero
was convicted of groping?

The town lost its luster.

What do magicians' assistants do if unemployed?

They turn tricks.

What do reluctant nice girls do if asked to give head?

Sooner or later, they succumb.

201

Did you hear about the patrolman who
didn't like skinny women?

He made the rounds.

202

Why are Nepali virgins scared of the
Abominable Snowman?

They say, "Himalayas!"

What research do fetishists like to read?

The footnotes.

What did the mortician give to his receptionist?

Funereal disease.

What did the musher's girlfriend like to eat?

His Idiot-a-rod.

What did the locksmith want from his sweetie?

A quick key.

What did the randy couple do in the bathroom?

They went into their "come-mode."

What did he do with the picture she sexted him?

Went virile.

209

Where do fetishists go for summer vacation?

Boot camp.

210

What did the dominatrix say about her costume?

"The pleather is all mine."

211

Which football players do some women avoid?

The tight end and the long snapper.

Assorted and Sordid

"Vary strange indeed; not for the Little Match Girl!"
~ ALLAN SUNDRY

Why do disgruntled employees attack
colleagues with sticky notes?
They "go Post-it."

Why do some people react mirthlessly to these puns?
They've out-groan them.

How do you finance a piss-poor higher education?
You use urine tuition!

215

How do robots reproduce?
By auto-mating.

216

What did the jailbird do with his smuggled "heater"?
He made smoked turkey.

217

Who is the police chief of Athens?
Orestes Perps.

218

How do you feel when you drop your
toothpaste on the floor?
Crestfallen.

219

How do you divide society into equal parts?
There are the halves and the halve-nots.

220

How do valedictorians break into the job market?

The make four A's.

221

What do professional beggars wear to work?

A coat of alms.

222

What stopped the contractor from building
a second housing development?

He had a one-tract mind.

223

What percentage of motel space is
occupied by deep thinkers?

One ruminate.

224

How do intellectuals travel to New Orleans?

They take the Tulane highway.

225

Why did the vandal trash the mausoleum?

He was very disturning.

226

How do you communicate an apology?

You use Remorse Code.

227

How did the man react to inheriting his uncle's old Jeep?

It gave him the Willys!

228

Why do hipsters prefer Casablanca?

It's a Moroccan place than most.

229

Why did they dump the voting booth in the harbor?

It contained secret ballast.

230

Did you hear about the seamstress who moonlighted as a hooker?

She was hemming and whoring.

231

Why don't supermarkets promote some cashiers?

They have checkered pasts.

232

Where do Cub Scouts sleep?

On boycotts.

233

What do you mostly see on a sharecrop farm?

Britches and boers.

234

What did the winner do in the Honda demolition derby?

Struck Accord.

235

What's the latest from the flag industry?

It had a banner year.

236

Why do some people cross-dress for business meetings?

They have hidden a gender.

237

What do DEA agents do for jollies?

They tell "narc-narc" jokes.

238

What do you call a retired auditor?

A has-been counter.

239

Who wanders the streets of Sudan?

Khartoum characters.

240

What happens in the streets of South Sudan?

Juba-lation.

241

Did you hear about the cross-dressing psychic?

She wore her trance vest tight.

242

What happens to those who don't blend in?

They get Oster-sized.

243

What language do clairvoyants use?

Farsi.

244

What do people do in long restroom lines?

They mind their pees and queues.

245

What did the shoplifter say to the pharmacist?
What's this pilfer?

246

Where do shopping addicts go for a recharge?
To the outlet mall.

247

What did the egotistical prosecutor harbor?
Delusions of grand jury.

248

Why did the woman gift-wrap rat poison for her ex?
As a toxin of her esteem.

249

How did the leper react to the jeering tourist?
Gave him the finger.

250

What does "diurnal" mean?

It's German for "le pissoir."

251

What's the biggest chain of car dealers in Istanbul?

The Automan Empire.

252

Why did the grammarian do laundry with his paramour?

They liked to dip-thongs.

253

How did the shoe repair shop corner the market?

They would not be under-soled.

254

How do C-minus students pay for study abroad?

They win Halfbright Fellowships.

255

Why did the witch skip her turn at the cauldron?

She wanted to rest a spell.

256

What do you tell someone hiding in a privy?

"Urine over your head."

257

Why did the couple have delusions of persecution?

They were a pair annoyed.

258

Why did the tree surgeon quit?

He got sycamore pruning.

259

What precipitated the riot in Singapore?

A wild Malay.

Malapropisms

A

"He began his **accent** up the corporate latter."
He rose from the guttural!

•

"I enjoy center stage and **acclimation**."
Better find an employer with an "open-window" policy, then.

•

"We all need water, sleep, and an **adamant** food supply."
You might have to go on a stead-fast.

•

"I will describe the interview with no further **adieu**."
By your leave, get into commotion!

•

"It was an **admiral** achievement for her."
She pierced her naval.

"In my small, rural town, there was no cultural **adversity**."
The hardship stayed at anchor.

•

"The idea was right down my **ally**."
We called him "Deep Throat."

•

"He came **along** way in his career."
He used the sidewalk the whole distance.

•

"Visitors are not **aloud** in the kitchen."
*They're not permitted to waste voluble time
or be the vocal point.*

•

"At 12 I became an **alter** boy."
That's when you started singing soprano.

•

"I love **analizing** data."
No doubt you're very retentive!

"Experience will be the **anecdote** to
my lack of self-confidence."
Call it: heads or tales?

•

"He used to be a financial **annalist**."
That's pretty much his story, now.

•

"I recall a funny **antidote**."
So let's take a walk down remedy lane.

•

"Early retirement is **apart** of my goal."
*It's great that you're concentrating only
on the core components.*

•

"He became an **armature** boxer and
won the Golden Gloves."
He generated enough interest to turn pro.

•

"At the startup phase of the business,
many problems **arouse**."
It's due to horning in on competitors.

"I can rapidly **asses** tricky situations."
It tax one to know one!

•

"I'm **ashy** guy."
Just like my old pallid, Wan Valdez!

•

"Airline **attendance** don't have as much free time."
Isn't showing up half the game?

•

"He was **augmentative**, and loved to debate."
He didn't need an amplifier!

•

"He once worked for **Author** Andersen."
He wore Hans-me downs.

•

"In her specialty, she's the world's leading **authoritarian**."
She makes a good first repression.

B

"I asked about her **back round**."
She said, "I never got over the hump."

•

"I enjoy **bailing** hay."
It must cost you a bundle, though.

•

"When the **ballet** measure passed,
her business was threatened."
She got the pointe.

•

"Things were going fine, then all at once
everything went **bamb**!"
Oh, deer!

•

"Her brother couldn't **bare** her presence."
He couldn't stand any more bad nudes.

"They **barley** get by."
They're malty-taskers.

•

"My younger brother ate **beatles**."
Not to mention yellow submarine sandwiches.

•

"My mother has **bee** my most positive influence."
She's a real honey.

•

"He went on to **beggar** and better triumphs."
He was mooch too successful to say farewell to alms.

•

"Opening the new store was the **begging** of the end!"
To beseech his own.

•

"I **bereted** myself for this mistake."
You were overcome with self-hat.

•

"At the auction, he triumphed with unemotional **biding**."
They made an offer he couldn't effuse.

"The Board meeting was a real nail **bitter**."
A tacky meal?

•

"What **blokes** the creative process from occurring?"
Tripping over guy-wires?

•

"Real business **bluffs** will enjoy this story."
They have deceits on the Stock Exchange.

•

"He had a **board** range of interests."
He sawed a wide scope of possibilities.

•

"She started by raising **boarder** collies."
Some were vicious roomers!

•

"Prosperity had returned, and the economy was **bombing**."
The newly rich vacationed in Grenade-a.

•

"He and his two **bothers** opened a new location."
One was a nerd, the other, annoyed.

"Ever the entrepreneur, he sought
to **brake** into new fields."
Such as slow gin and ice-cream stoppings?

•

"Her skill is **brining** a product to market."
When she finds a dilly, she doesn't dally.

•

"He is on the go, a very **busing** man."
He's very driven; he used to be in training.

•

"I worked my way through school as a **buss** boy."
I gave them a lot of lip.

•

"Put two stubborn people together
and they **butt-heads**."
Don't tell asshole.

•

"Then, a year went **buy**."
It was a week economy.

C

"There are three kinds of learners: auditory,
visual, and **callisthenic**."
You are tendon to jump to conclusions!

•

"He loves his **carrier**, and can't wait to go to work."
Perhaps he's with UPS?

•

"In the restaurant trade, you need common **cents**."
It's inherited from your penny Auntie.

•

"This economy is **chalk** full of surprises."
It makes one blanch.

•

"With women, he's Prince **Charmer**."
He drives a Cobra.

"Getty was so **cheep,** he had a payphone in his lobby."
He liked robin friends of their quarters.

•

"Summers, he works at **cheery** harvesting."
He sings: "High-hoe, high-hoe," even when he's in the pits.

•

"He took very unconventional routes to **chive** his goals."
He made certain that there were no leeks to the press.

•

"They need to **clam** down, to solve their problems."
You can't help others if you're shellfish!
Don't stick your Littleneck out.

•

"I was one of a small **cliché** of friends."
They were thick as thieves, birds of a feather…

•

"Through the years, she remains my **closet** friend."
You've had many clothes encounters.

•

"I **cold** have an effect on society."
You might be The Big Chill.

"I excelled, and was admitted to the **collage** of my choice."
You paste up and down the halls of ivy.

•

"I keep my **composer** at all times."
Bach then, you were Haydn from the truth.

•

"My co-workers **compromise** my greatest influences."
They take in, and give in.

•

"How **con** you live without humor?"
You might consult Dr. Fraud.

•

"My happiness is what counts, even though
this may sound **conceded**."
Granted, you stuck-up for yourself.

•

"Feeling trapped, he wanted to get out of his **confides**."
They were bound to secrecy.

•

"I'd like to open a chain of **connivance** stores, like 7-11."
I'll abet you do!

"The bickering family members should go see a **consular**."
They can charge the sessions to their visa card.

•

"At funerals, he **consuls** everybody."
He helps them to envoy the moment.

•

"He **contributed** his workaholism to the example
set by his father."
*His dad told him: "I gave at the office, so whistle
while you quirk!"*

•

"Our family home is in a **cool-a-sack**."
Your Popsicle built it.

•

"The idea struck a **cord**."
"Oh dear, I severed your lifeline," said Tom, atonally.

•

"After high school, he joined the Marine **Core**."
*His unit was in the upper crust, but
bad apples surrounded him.*

"Group projects in this company require
lots of **corporation**."
Wouldn't partnership be a better form?

•

"She wants to stay on the west **cost**."
That could be occidentally expensive.

•

"Remember: the **costume**r is always right!"
All the world's a stage.

•

"He served his **county** by joining the Marines."
He fought globally, thought locally.

•

"His first job was cleaning a chicken **coup**."
There was no thrill of the junta.

•

"I don't like to **cow-tow** to bosses."
*You can tow a cow to warder, but you can
only say tusk-tusk to a sycophant.*

"I like to make decorations: I am **crafty**."
You wile away the hours.

•

"He used his ingenuity to **crate** a new product."
He thought outside the box!

•

"The shop appealed to the fast-lane **crowed**."
They had caws to pack the place.

•

"They spend all day in their **cubical**."
They've developed a bad sphere of confinement;
they want to be well rounded.

•

"The speaker made numerous off the **cusp** remarks."
His spurt-of-the-moment talks missed the point.

D

"My grandfather's **dearth** was unexpected."
His lack ran out.

•

"Orpheus made a **decent,** to rescue his wife."
He went down, in an upright manner.

•

"There was a **defiant** pattern to the increase in revenue."
It resists explanation.

•

"I inherited his **defuse** traits."
We were like appease in a pod.

•

"He makes **descent** wages."
That's because he works for Dad.

"Most of all, I love being in the high **dessert**."
What was in those brownies, anyway?

•

"Adversity didn't **detour** him from new ventures."
He got to the route of problems.

•

"He was definitely a **diffident** entrepreneur
from all the other ones."
He was shy – about one brick's worth.

•

"Napoleon had **diluted** ideas."
He said: "I'm hallucinating about water, Lou."

•

"She was **ding** her best."
Now, why does that ring a bell?

•

"I am good at leading a **discourse** group
of people to harmony."
You commune with them every Sundry.

"He quickly **dissembles** guns."
He's a real (water) pistol!

•

"She works for the local school **distract**."
She gives diverts students detour.

•

"I take time out after a hard day to **distress**."
I'm pain for meditation lessons.

•

"I lacked the **dive** for knowledge until now."
You'd steered past the bar.

•

"He earned his **doctrine** of philosophy at Wisconsin."
Still, he was a loose canon: "Love him, love his dogma."

•

"In that business, there's never a **dole** moment."
The competition gives no quarter.

•

"Hard work **dose** not bother me."
It's just the prescription.

"He seems a **downed to earth** kind of guy."
He's taking crash courses.

•

"He came from a poor family, which had
to **make due** with little."
Their mantra was "owe-owe!"

•

"Getty **dyed** alone."
He succumbed to his own off-color story.

E

"Wally Amos regretted ignoring his sons **earier** in life."
Back then, he lacked sound judgment.

•

"The rogue trader was sentenced to 6 **ears** in jail."
Further, he was fined a buccaneer.

•

"She wears dangly **earnings**."
Face it: we're in a lobal economy.

•

"This company **empathized** teamwork."
They stressed being vicarious over the competition.

•

"To instill a work ethic, his dad **ebbed** him on
by matching his allowance."
"If at first you don't recede…"

"Junior was the latest **edition** to the family."
"Extra, extra, read all about it!"

•

"I found employment **else ware**."
It's a no-name deep-discount chain.

•

"He is the **epiphany** of an entrepreneur."
He keeps up appearances, to the highest degree.

•

"She felt the **erg** to ask deep questions
about the business."
She was dyne to stay current.

•

"Without **evening** stopping to think …"
He plugged in his new Dusk-buster.

•

"Recently, he was **evolved** in automotive sales."
Before, he was a grease monkey.

•

"J. Paul Getty wanted to be socially **excepted**."
So he founded "Lepers Anonymous" as his omission in life.

"Most clients are friendly, **except for a few exceptions**."
Such as those with redundant redundancies?

•

"The injury **exemplified** him from serving in the Army."
Nonetheless, he went on to become Precedent.

•

"I will quote an **exert** from the book."
With great effort, you've found the secret passage.

•

"She kept **expending** her business."
It grew into nothingness.

•

"He is an **expertise** in his field."
He's a master baiter.

F

"He closed his auto **factors**, leaving many
people unemployed."
"Elementary, my dear Datsun."

•

"I hope that I **fair** well in my career."
Just beware of carnival pleasures.

•

"He went on to meet a grim **fait**."
One might say it was "accompli."

•

"I plan to **fallow** the yellow brick road to success."
*You won't seed Oz very fast, and you may have
harrowing experiences. So, cut out the crop!*

•

"She praised me, which I found very **faltering**."
And she wavered to you in the hallway.

"It's not **fare** to judge people."
I toll you not to get charged up when you're ticketed off.

•

"I want to work for a company that will show
me all the **fascists** of the job."
That's a gem of an idea, though it might raise a Führer.

•

"It made me **feal** peculiar."
A sinking sensation, as on a leaky vassal?

•

"I can't tell what the **feature** holds."
Maybe you should watch the coming attractions.

•

"Those were big shoes to **feel**."
They were cut for Bunyans.

•

"She had accomplished an amazing **feet**."
It was the sole reason for her heeling.

•

"He is a real sports **feign,** especially NBA."
Could have fooled me.

"He **fells** a strong sense of social justice."
His views are clear-cut.

●

"Cinderella is a well-known **ferry tail**."
Boat her sisters treated her like ship!

●

"She doubled sales, a formidable **fete**."
She did it by following the party line.

●

"She made it through her obstacles with
the support of her **fiends**."
They brought her deviled eggs and bowls of cruel.

●

"We need a level playing **filed**."
Rasp and you shall get.

●

"She is the proud **finance** of the owner."
He needs her dowry to keep up with the Dow-Joneses.
She thinks that he looks good invests.

"She **finely** found success."
In the end, the answer was with thin.

•

"He has **finical** expertise."
He keeps a fuss-budget.

•

"She makes a good **firs** impression."
She could spruce up her coniferences by serving logger beer.

•

"He **fist** started in business in 1972."
By now, he's punch-drunk.

•

"My brother was ill with the **flew**."
He was sore from being crouped up.

•

"He assumed **fool** ownership of the company."
He was jester risk-taker.

•

"His uncle was a liar and **fore**-flusher."
He said, "I'll sewer you for all you have!"

"Their business had nowhere to go but **foreword**."
They'd already lost their appendix.

•

"They were **formally** the owners of a
successful restaurant."
They used to cater to large conventions.

•

"I'll never forget **forth** grade."
Was that when you left the Third World?

•

"I have many **found** memories of childhood."
You've stopped drinking milk of amnesia.

•

"He has a **fowl** temper!"
He's enraged by the most poultry remark.

•

"They examined the major **frets** to the corporation."
Many were in the key of A-menace.

G

"Their shoes are designed to fit runners' **gates**."
They said, "It pace to come in here."

•

"He began in timber with **George of** Pacific."
Formerly of The Jungle?

•

"His parents gave him a **gob**."
It was a closeout sail-or.

•

"They call her a **goody-too-shoes**."
But her friends still call her Imelda!

•

"I never take things for **granite**."
Will marbles never cease?

"Last year, the firm suffered **grater** losses."
It barely scraped by.

•

"He put his nose to the **grind**."
Except when stoned, he was a whet blanket.

•

"I admired his **gross** attention to detail."
He does boor-ing work.

•

"Integrity is his major **guildline**."
It didn't league him astray.

•

"He had the **gull** to open a clothing store
next door to his competitor."
He prospered by deceit of his pants.

H

"Her mother is a very **had** worker."
She's an exploit witness!

•

"At Agincourt, the troops were rallied by **Hamlet**."
*In his small-town manner, he spoke softly but carried
a fall staff. (He was a Hal fellow well met.)*

•

"He was a slave driver, inspiring his staff to work **hardly**."
They made themselves scarce.

•

"**Hark** work pays off!"
A slacker can lose his heed.

•

"To guarantee my appointment, I phoned a **head**."
We joint forces.

"I fell head over **heals**."
I had too much ail, then footed the bill.

•

"I'd like to be the **heard** golf pro at a good course."
You'll need to develop a sound game.

•

"Expansion of the business was a fool-**hearty** idea."
Jest was too offbeat.

•

"Donald Trump built a Manhattan landmark,
the Grand **Height** Hotel."
He liked to weave tall stories.

•

"She is the **heroin** of her own life story."
But she can take being needled.

•

"They prefer to **higher** college students."
Only upper-division?

•

"The town had a nice, **homely** feel."
It was out on the plains.

"Realtors need to know all about **hoses**."
If they don't, their sales can go down the tube.

•

"He was two-faced, terribly **hypercritical**."
He was full of carp!

I

"I made **immense** for my mistakes."
Must have been enormous ones.

•

"I admired him, and wanted to **immolate** him."
A burning desire?

•

"My teachers **impounded** rules into my mind."
You used to be towheaded.

•

"He ignored his son's **impute**."
He said: "Why do I need data? I already have ascribe."

•

"He **indulged** some private financial information to me."
He was gone with the whim.

"I can't see myself **inhibiting** that field."
Don't dwell on it; you make a lasting first repression.

•

"This gave me an **inside** into his motives."
He had an interiority complex.

•

"His parents **installed** good ideas in him."
No wonder he's always loaded!

•

"As a child, she was shy and **inverted**."
Too many headstands will do that to you.

•

"He has worked at the same company for **ions**."
He's known for his up-and-atom approach.

•

"Teens are reckless because they think they're **invisible**."
Out of sight, out of mind.

•

"I want him to walk me down the **isle**."
As long as your dress isn't maroon.

J

"He loves his **Job**."
He's a trial lawyer.

•

"She **jut** jumped into opening the business,
without thinking."
She was quickly overextended.

K

"They tried to **ketch** up to the competition."
They mast their forces.

•

"After his divorce, Citizen Kane lived with **know one**."
He left Welles enough alone and got him to a none-ry.

L

"He worked his way up the **latter**."
He rung his only competitor's neck.

•

"He specializes in business **law suits**."
He said, "Go vest young man."

•

"He aspires to be a DA or an environmental **layer**."
They're a varnishing species.

•

"He **lead** his company for 50 years."
It was a heavy act to follow.

•

"I will use what I **leaned** in this class."
If you're so inclined. Now visit Pisa.

"I want to move to a higher **lever**."
You want to eat cake, instead of being left only the fulcrums.

•

"Their roles **lied** in both the family and business areas."
They reclined to take an oath.

•

"Their strict rules were for **ligament** reasons."
Still, they were tendon to be broken.

•

"In that business, you have **limed** options."
There's more than one way tequila cat.

•

"He's very good at **listing** to others' ideas."
That's how he founded his coffee company, "Starboard."

•

"I learned a **lit** of new ideas."
I studied with skillful arsonists.

•

"He **lobbed** the bankers for a new loan."
He made his pitch, but it bombed.

"I admired him; he has the heart of a **loin**."
He plays his haunches.

•

"He's always **loosing** things."
He likes wanton soup, but he lax insight.

•

"He's a highly **lucrative** person."
He's a profit with honor.

M

"My skills **mach** up well with his."
Your minds are constantly racing.

•

"My two major influences were my mom and my **mad**."
Irate him highly.

•

"He grew up in **Main**."
Down East, he was a real gas!

•

"The store employs a non-family **manger**."
He's a straw boss.

•

"She runs the firm in a smooth **manor**."
She's in estate of bliss, building castles in the air.

"I must **marinate** my skills at a high level."
"A mind is a terrible thing to baste."

●

"Grandpa was a good **markers** man."
He was a straight shooter, right up to his debt.

●

"My breakthrough is just a **mater** of time."
Mom's the word.

●

"Her talents **math** mine well."
That sums it up.

●

"Oregon is his alma **matter**."
It was there that he learned substance abuse.

●

"I liked her from the moment we **meant**."
She became my main source of purport.

●

"She makes jewelry from pliable **medals**."
She's award of the state.

"He led a balanced life, a happy **median**."
The grass was greener there.

•

"I need to **melt** my talents with my values."
You'll be among the chosen fuse, like the merge-gent of Venice.

•

"My **miner** is sociology."
That's a good field for a stoner.

•

"I lived five **minuets** from school."
It was just a short waltz.

•

"Sometimes I **miss** understand."
It left without reason.

•

"He worked for the **mobile** oil corporation."
He liked to "go with the flow."

•

"The prosecutor spoke in a calm and **modern** tone."
He had a recent opinion of himself.

"This career would provide me with
big **monitory** rewards."
As long as you haven't warn out your welcome.

•

"When I'm sad, I tend to **mop**."
You turn pail.

•

"She played the **moroccos** in the jazz band."
She liked the theme from "Casablanca."

•

"Not knowing English, I struggled for a few **moths**."
Where there's a wool, there's a way.

N

"After college, he earned his **NBA**."
It was a tall order.

•

"I'll be employed for the **nest** three months."
You took the fledge of allegiance.

•

"Sir Gawain was challenged by the Green **Night**."
Then he took off his shades, and they duked it out.

•

"It's a tightly **nit** group of managers."
They hang around the water cooler, spinning lousy yarns and being picky.

•

"I must find a **nitch** to pursue."
You can scratch that idea!

"She had in **numeral** plans in her head for new products."

Her daze was numbered?

"They work too many **ours**."
Especially the "we small ours."

•

"I keep an **opened** mind."
Igor delivered it one night.

•

"She was **opnoxious** to everybody."
Her modern art made them want to barf.

•

"I was **ounce** in that position myself."
But time weights for no one.

•

"The company serves the city and **outlining** areas."
Its suburban data are sketchy.

"The benefits **out way** the risks."
It's the route, if you want to exceed.

•

"Someone **overhead** my plan."
He was on a rafter – without a paddle.

•

"She **overseas** the advertising department."
She supervises the junket mail.

•

"I want to work **oversees** for a while."
You want to supervise foreign wide. It'll Legree with you.

P

"My achievements **pail** before hers."
There's more than wan way to urn respect.

•

"A chef needs a refined **palette**."
Avoid off-color yolks.

•

"She and I were an unlikely **paring**."
You had adjacent cuticles.

•

"I enjoy many **pass times**."
Your favorite is Monday Night Football.

•

"In 1985, his father **pasted** away."
They stuck him in the ground.

"It takes lots of **patients** to design clothing."
Sometimes you have to doctor up a Band-Aid
solution, even if it turns out invalid.

•

"This **patter** would recur in his life."
It sometimes spieled trouble.

•

"As a child, she loved to **pay** with clay."
Now, for fun, she launders her money.

•

"His business card has flower **pedals** on it."
He wheels and deals roses.

•

"This information **peeked** my curiosity."
I joined a peer group.

•

"In times of trouble, you must **perceiver**
until you break through."
Sees the day!

"At first, he cold-called **perspective** customers."
Alas, most of them saw only through a glass, darkly.

●

"A high GPA is a **perquisite** to a good job."
It's mandatory; make no bonus about it.

●

"He decided not to **peruse** starting a new career."
He didn't walk the stalk.

●

"He attends the University of **Peugeot** Sound."
His parents pay a grand prix for tuition.

●

"J. Paul Getty amassed a fortune, letting
nothing **phase** him."
He knew that all the world's a stage.

●

"The payoff of keeping the business in the
family was **piece** of mind."
I'm partial to that.

"At this **pint,** I made a major decision."
Hope you didn't decide to drive.

●

"He **plains** to work on Wall Street."
He's taken a flat nearby.

●

"His consultations are well **planed.**"
He does them in the buff.

●

"I love jumping out of **plans.**"
"Oh, chute!"

●

"Social problems **plaque** the nation."
We're down to the skin of our teeth.

●

"She used to work in a manufacturing **plat.**"
At the factory, she had a one-tract mind.

●

"I spent my spare time **plying** football."
Now, you're left with your laminations.

"This **poises** the question: is outside experience desirable?"
The answer, which hangs in the balance, is indeed propound.

•

"I **posses** those skills, too."
Cut 'em off at the pass!

•

"The bully **prayed** on weaker kids."
He devoured their school lunches, by hymn-self.

•

"It was a **prefect** day to start on a trip."
When in Rome, do as the roamers do.

•

"He was promoted to the position of **Present**."
He lorded it over the absentees.

•

"Her **presents** lift my spirits."
You have the gift of grab.

•

"He had ample **prier** experience in the industry."
He formerly wrote a gossip column.

"She's now the vice **principle** at the school."
She walks around in scandals.

●

"I revealed my most **privet** secrets."
You didn't beat around the bush.

●

"He researched **pubicly** held companies."
He had them by the short hairs, but it was lousy work.

●

"I wonder what path to **purse**."
You could try shadowing a bag lady.

Q

"Personalities can be divided into the four **quadroons**."
But be careful, while classifying, not to fold,
spindle, or mulatto.

•

"He **quiet** his job to start his own company."
He was a silent partner.

•

"I sang in the **quire**."
No improv allowed; strictly by the book.

R

"She **rally** enjoys her garden."
She sings: "Kale, kale, the gang's all here!"

•

"When his dad retired, he took over and **rant** the shop."
It received rave reviews.

•

"I **rapped** my car around a tree."
"It split in two, I said words of blue, what could I do?"

•

"His brother was a convicted **rappist**."
He went to the school of hard knocks.

•

"He is the top home-seller for a **reality** company."
No field of dreams in his inventory!

"Do not let anything cloud your **reams**."
Your aspirations can be boring!

•

"Wally Amos capitalized on his aunt's
delicious cookie **receipt**."
"Add sugar and flour to paper, bake slowly."

•

"They **reeked** the benefits of their work."
Their smell business grew.

•

"She **refereed** me to one of her suppliers."
She was ump-pathetic.

•

"She keeps a strict **regiment** at the office."
The dreaded diet-corporals.

•

"My teachers gave me free **reign**."
They knuckled under to a ruler.

•

"**Relaters** are paid only if they sell property."
They seek narrates of return.

"It's **relativity** hard to grow a business."
It takes a real Einstein, who was a germane.

•

"She **relays** on her clients."
She keeps track of the ones in Baton Rouge.

•

"Meditation helps to **relive** his depression."
It's déjà blue all over again.

•

"You should **rely** bad news tactfully."
Pass it on, before they go off the depend.

•

"She has excellent **report** with her staff."
From here to affinity, by all accounts.

•

"If he were caught, the government
would **reprimand** his assets."
He'd be in Witness Protection in Rebuke, Iowa.

•

"She used to work as a **respitory** therapist."
It was only for a breathe interval.

"After working at Subway, I want to open
my own **restraint.**"
Where they serve fasten food.

●

"He contracted a **retched** ailment."
It's such a sad story – no gags, please.

●

"He **reveled** to the class that he
had been a juvenile delinquent."
Maybe he was disclosing his "party of the first part"?

●

"The personality inventory at last **reviled** my true talents."
They showed you detest.

●

"Our different viewpoints have caused some **riffs**."
They don't jive with one another.

●

"College is a **right of passage**."
So is peristalsis.

"Leadership of the company was his birth **rite**."
He stood on his ceremony.

•

"He was a great **roll** model."
The original Pillsbury Doughboy?

•

"She was very **rood** to my other friends."
She talked at cross-purposes.

•

"He was a **rouged** individualist."
Until he was caught red-handed.

•

"There's no map to the **rout** of life."
It helps to read the beat poets.

•

"The family farm can have some **ruff** times."
Of coarse, some grow collared greens.

•

"The corporate game plan went a **rye**."
Served, no doubt, with a twist of lemon?

S

"He has a **said** story to tell."
When he only hummed it, nobody listened.

•

"Dharma is a word from **sand** script."
It was originally in the polish language.

•

"I was taught that **Satin** lurks everywhere."
He may be smooth, but he's no man of the cloth!

•

"Buying and selling real estate can
be a pain **sating** process."
"The assuages of sin are deft."

•

"Her help was a life-**savor**."
Life is a taste; may you pass it!

"I was born in **Scared** Heart Hospital."
Where birthing and cardiac are combined
into one department.

•

"She was **scarred** of her own power."
She said: "Taint no fun to be dread to the world, 'zit?"

•

"Joe Keller broke the laws, but blamed his partner,
and got off **Scotch-free**."
The court was in The Haig.

•

"He **scrapped** together some money for his new venture."
From junk bonds, no doubt.

•

"They **seam** to work well as a unit."
Actually, they're only sew-sew.

•

"Our team was **seated** only seventh in the tournament."
So, we took a strong stand.

"He didn't need a lot of capital to **secede** in business."
He needed only a Dixie cup.

•

"She said, as we parted, 'I'll **seem** you later.'"
Just keeping up appearances?

•

"This never **seizes** to amaze me."
It's endless what can grab you.

•

"From the start, they were highly **self-efficient**."
They compared amples to origins.

•

"Ever **sense** high school, she wanted to open a business."
In the interim, she relied on intuition.

•

"His father was a **sever** alcoholic."
It's best not to axe about him (or his sister, Maim).

•

"Scrooge was visited by **severable** ghosts."
He thought he'd taken cleave of his census.

"I'm seeking **shear** satisfaction in a career."
Perhaps work for Cutter Labs?

●

"Their confidence **shinned** through."
"Tibia or not tibia, that was the question."

●

"He looked to be a **shoe-in** for the position."
But then he put his foot in his mouth.

●

"If employees fail to **shoe-up,** the manager must cover."
He socks it to them!

●

"I drank bad coffee and **shuttered!**"
You trembled like a batten the belfry.

●

"I become easily **side-tract**."
You don't digest the facts.

●

"She didn't have a **signal** hair out of place."
It's gesture mousse at work again.

"I can **sill** remember my first customer."
He arrived just as you were ready to jump.

•

"She had a **since** of inner peace."
Déjà vu strikes again?

•

"He **singed** a non-compete contract."
It was his biggest scorch.

•

"I hate the **site** of blood."
Looks as if your medical career is in vein.

•

"He water **skies** daily."
They call him The Rainmaker.

•

"He **sled** in and out of relationships."
They were all runners or dogs.

•

"How would you like sand **slug** on you by a bully?"
It cam to pass on Mussel Beach.

"He retired, due to a **soar** back."
His medical costs went through the roof.

•

"He was born in **Sol**, Korea."
He definitely wasn't a Moonie.

•

"The company was profitable only for a **sort** period."
Then it hit arrange of losses.

•

"Her mother gained **soul** custody of her."
The judge said, "That's the spirit!"

•

"Scrooge, led by the **sprits**, had a transformation."
He tried to spar with them, but then
bowed to their stern commandments.

•

"I made a pain **staking** effort."
"Take, that, Dracula!"

"She **stared** her own ad agency."
She initially wanted the glare of publicity,
but not the gapes of wrath.

•

"I applied only to **stated** universities."
The unstated ones are hard to find, anyway.

•

"It was about the takeover of a **steal** company."
They made an iron pilfer everyone.

•

"At age 75, he **stills** works every day."
He labors until the moonshine comes out.

•

"They **stove** to attain customer loyalty."
They endeavored to be in at the kiln.

•

"His business dealings were **strait** forward."
Except when he veered into the impassing lane.

•

"I **stride** to achieve."
May you triumph, pacefully.

"This career **suites** her fine."
(*Especially the upscale accommodations.*)

•

"He is the **super-intend-ant**."
He leads the weak-willed short-termites.

•

"I found that my momentary fear had **surpassed**."
You ended up in the Great Beyond.

•

"I had this bitter-**sweat** feeling."
Dank's a lot!

T

"He was stuck at one level, because he lacked **tack**."
They said, "Brad, we get your gauche."

•

"Trump called his casino the **Tajma Hall**."
The name Agra-vated some people.

•

"I like to **talk** care of animals."
Try a job at a chat house.

•

"Not **tall** the children joined the family business."
Only those with nothing Toulouse.

•

"Instead of services, I prefer to sell a **tangle** product."
Don't be touchy – or snarl at the customers.

"Jackie Robinson **tarnished** the color barrier."
He showed his metal.

•

"She runs her company on a **taught** little budget."
She's learned how to string along her creditors.

•

"My parents **taut** me good work habits."
Learning from them was a real stretch,
but you were tight friends.

•

"His best skill is being **tedious** at bookkeeping."
Such weary debits!

•

"He found his first job though a **tempt** agency."
It's called Lure-Id and Associates.

•

"He didn't get **ten-year** at his first teaching job."
Must have been the 7-year itch!

•

"I went in and spoke to **thee** entrepreneur."
Thou sayst?

"A former actress, she started a **theoretical** company."
It performed Noh plays.

•

"My parents **thought** me all that I know."
They named me Inkling.

•

"Henry V claimed the **thrown**."
He played "catch as catch can."

•

"Henry IV didn't **thrust** his son, Hal."
Otherwise, there would have been no Henry V.

•

"She used her family **tides** to get ahead."
She wasn't afraid to make waves.

•

"He was **tiered** of working for someone else."
So he and his boss had a row.

•

"She **tired** to conduct efficient meetings."
She wondered if the endeavor would come,
or if she'd exhausted the possibilities.

"He is known as a critical **tinker**."
He often calls the kettle black!

•

"Her hobby is **toll** painting."
Wooden you know, she does it just for change.

•

"I learned a lot from interviewing **Tome**."
You could read him like a book.

•

"I don't like to **tot** my own horn."
I can't blare to. (Just "kidding"!)

•

"I learn through **trail** and error."
Sounds path-etic.

•

"She works hard and is good at her **trait**."
She's attribute to her profession.

•

"She operates from **tree** main beliefs."
They are: branch out, root out competition, and log on.

"She can't see the forest for the **tress**."
Hair today, gone tomorrow.

•

"I want a career that's full of **trills**."
Be careful you don't end up in Sing-Sing.

•

"She stuck with it, **trough** thick and thin."
She went from hollow to goodbye.

•

"I had many different **Tudors** in English."
The fat guy with six wives was the best.

•

"He's a **tuff** boss."
Subject to frequent eruptions.

•

"Applying to college was the **tuning** point of my life."
You'll refrain from saying more, not wanting to put on airs.

•

"I watch mystery shows to guess the **turnout**."
You want to see how many done it.

U

"She was inexperienced, so the CEO took
her **under his shoulder**."
It was the pits.

•

"Orpheus descended to the **under-word**."
Dropping his Webster's behind him, he fled to the Styx.

•

"His leadership **untied** people in his profession."
He helped the have-knots.

V

"My personal **vales** are mostly traditional ones."
Well, that's no reason for depression.

•

"I want to be a great entrepreneur, like **Vanderbuilt**."
You can manufacture commode-doors.

•

"Her openness left her **venerable** to criticism."
She lets off esteem once a weak.

•

"In England, a minister is called "the **victor**."
But the losers say "Parish the thought!"

•

"Awful things happen to bad people, and **visa** versa."
This too shall pass?

"He has a **viscous** temper."
His evil moods pus him in some sticky situations.

•

"They sell overseas and **vise** versa."
It creates a profit squeeze.

•

"The grandparents had **vitiation** rights."
The impair of them dropped in often.

"To induce her, the company **waived** money at her."
It was a haunting refrain.

•

"At work, he **wares suites**."
He's formal, to say the lease.

•

"This is a business **wear** the employees feel comfortable."
Especially on "Casual Fridays."

•

"He's conservative, and **weary** of anything new."
Having exhausted corporate resources,
he's now Chary of the Board.

•

"Management must decide **weather** to grow the company."
They're consulting the meteorologist from
the Extension Service.

"He had a domineering mother and a **week** father."
Dad walked around in a days.

•

"The bistro is famous for its **weight** staff."
The chef said, "Menu must lay off the desserts!"

•

"He sells **wenches** for model airplanes."
They may be comely, but they tend to bolt.

•

"He was a **whinny** crybaby."
It left him quite horse, and he smelled like Pooh.

•

"They support me **whit** their friendship."
I've come to 'speck it.

•

"He was a **whole seller**."
Unlike the party of the first part.

•

"I regret how I treated her **wholeheatedly**."
When I let my frenzy my remorse, she said: "Cool!"

"The store has elaborately decorated **widows**."
In different shades of black.

•

"I like the **wine** of a turbo engine."
You like your gasket of amontillado.

•

"He's happy **wit** his lot."
He makes intriguing prepositions.

•

"I'm not sure **witch** career to choose."
You could be the saucier's apprentice.

•

"He **wondered** his path for years."
Sometimes he had amble doubt.

•

"I ran a stop sign and was cited for **wreckless** driving."
The police view you as a crash cow.

Made in the USA
Las Vegas, NV
22 December 2020